T0381217

Bryan's Special Bear

Written by: Janet Matthews
Illustrated by: Abednego Rodriguez

AuthorHouse™
1663 Liberty Drive
Bloomington, IN 47403
www.authorhouse.com
Phone: 1 (800) 839-8640

Published by AuthorHouse 12/11/2015

ISBN: 978-1-5049-6572-9 (sc)
ISBN: 978-1-5049-6856-0 (hc)
ISBN: 978-1-5049-6672-6 (e)

Library of Congress Control Number: 2015920470

Print information available on the last page.

This book is printed on acid-free paper.

Written for my First Grandbaby out of Love and Affection.
I hope you get as much enjoyment out of this story as I did writing it for you.

You will always be loved "Lots and Lots of Whole, Whole Bunches!!"

Love you forever,

Grandma Janet!

Once upon a time, a very Special bear was born.

He was special because God made him for a Special baby boy named Bryan.

Bryan's Mommy was shopping one day and saw this little bear just waiting for her to take him home. He was all dressed up in his very best bow!

Bear was so happy to be going to meet Bryan that he was singing his song all the way home.

He couldn't wait to play outside with Bryan, have a picnic, and make him smile! His song was about a picnic Bear wanted to have with his special little boy.

Bryan and his little Bear went everywhere together and when he got sleepy, Bear would sing his Special song and help him go to sleep so he would have sweet dreams.

Bear and Bryan had many picnics and good times but time went by so fast. Bryan was growing up and Bear was left behind more and more. This made him sad because he learned so much about the great big world when they were together!

He thought how fun it would be to go exploring. So he set out on an adventure.

The Bear went out to learn all he could about all the places he would like to go with Bryan.

He went to the sea where the beach was white and the sun shined bright.

He played in the sand but it just wasn't the same because Bryan wasn't there.

Bear went to the Circus, he wanted to share his cotton candy with Bryan, but he wasn't there. This made Bear very sad.

Bear heard that Bryan was growing up even bigger and had to go to school away from home. Bear said, "I should be there! Who will look after him?"

Bear was trying to find Bryan, he had moved away from where they lived together. Where is he going to search? Which direction should he go?

He is going to need help, but who will help him?

He searched and searched, from the mountains to the seas, from the hills to the desert. He didn't find him.

Bryan was no where to be found. Again Bear was sad.
"Where is my little boy?"

Years went by and Bryan forgot about Bear.

He was all grown up now. Would he remember his special little Bear?

How was he ever going to find him.

Bear searched and searched and searched.

Then.....

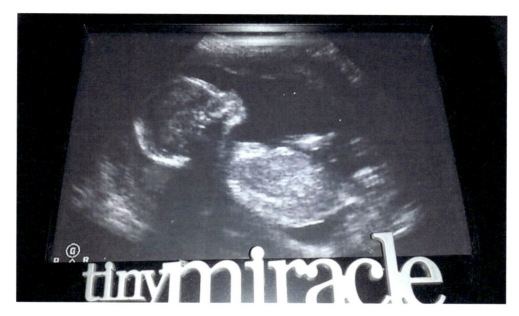

Bear got some news that made him jump for joy. There is going to be another little Bryan. "Oh no!" said Bear, "I have to find him. I have to sing him my special song."

"I have to be there for him to sing him to sleep and help him dream about our Picnics?"

Bear learned about computers and the internet! "This is a wonderful new way to search. I have to find Bryan now!" Bear said. He stayed up all night long trying, but Bear was getting very sleepy. He couldn't stay awake any longer so he decided to go to bed...

first he had to say his prayers.

He remembered how Bryan's Mommy found him in the store so he prayed to God to guide him back to his little boy, even if he was not a little boy anymore. He has to find him because God's plan was for Bryan and Bear to be together forever. God would know where Bryan is!

"Lord, I know you can find Bryan for me. You made me for him and I was not always there while he was growing up. I hope he will forgive me and let me be there for his new little boy. I promise, Lord, I will be there for him. I will not go on any more adventures. Please, Lord, help me find him!

In Jesus name, Amen!"

Bryan's mommy never forgot about Bear.

So as he slept, God went to work to answer his prayer.

After he prayed, God told Bryan's mommy to look for Bear too.

She looked on the internet for Bear and was so excited. Now she was jumping for Joy!

She found him!!!!!

She asked them, "Please make sure he gets home safe. Bear has to be here for when the new little boy comes".

Bryan's mommy welcomed Bear with a GREAT BIG Bear Hug, even though he is a little bear.

She promised Bear he will see his Bryan very soon but the new little Bryan has not arrived yet.

We have to wait for the Stork, you see, the truck that brought Bear home may have driven very fast but the Stork doesn't fly fast.

Especially when he is carrying Special little boys.

Bear was born: 1983

Bryan was born: 1984

Bear came home: February 19, 2015

Bear sees Bryan again and meets Mommy Keri: March 21, 2015

Bear meets his new little boy, Jacob: May 19, 2015

Bear is home forever!!!!

THE END

Printed in the United States
By Bookmasters